Getting To Know...

Nature's Children

CANADA GEESE

Judy Ross

SCHOLASTIC INC.

New York Toronto London Auckland Sydney
Mexico City New Delhi Hong Kong Buenos Aires

Facts in Brief

Classification of the Canada Goose

     Class: *Aves* (birds)

     Order: *Anseriformes* (duck-shaped waterfowl)

     Family: *Antidae* (surface duck family)

     Genus: *Branta*

     Species: *Branta canadensis*

World distribution. Native to North America, but has been introduced to Europe; found seasonally from the Arctic Ocean to Mexico.

Habitat. Marshy areas, ponds, streams, lake shallows.

Distinctive physical characteristics. Broad white band across throat and cheeks; black head, neck, legs, and feet.

Habits. Pairs for life; group migration in "V" formation to South for winter; well-developed communication signals.

Diet. Water plants, grasses, grain, insects.

Published by Scholastic Inc.
90 Old Sherman Turnpike, Danbury, Connecticut 06816.

SCHOLASTIC and associated logos are trademarks and/or registered trademarks of Scholastic Inc.

ISBN: 0-7172-7741-0   Printed in the U.S.A.

Edited by: Elizabeth Grace Zuraw   *Photo Editor:* Nancy Norton
Photo Rights: Ivy Images   *Cover Design:* Niemand Design

Have you ever wondered . . .

Have you ever been on a "wild goose chase"? That's when you run around chasing after something and never find it. The expression comes from pioneer days when settlers tried to catch a goose to eat. Geese are pretty clever and swift, so often the hunters would come home empty-handed after a long "wild goose chase."

When you think of a goose you may also think of the pictures of Mother Goose in your favorite book of nursery rhymes. The Canada Goose looks quite different. It has a plump gray body and a black neck and head with white patches on its cheeks. (And, of course, it doesn't wear a Mother Goose bonnet!) It does have a very long neck that can twist around in all directions. If you ever see a gooseneck lamp, you'll know where that name came from.

Most people see Canada Geese only when the birds fly overhead honking loudly. Now let's take a closer look at these beautiful creatures.

A male Canada Goose proudly displays his handsome markings.

Splish, Splash!

Do you like taking baths? If you do, you have something in common with Canada Geese. Even baby geese enjoy bathtime. They plop into the water with their parents on a hot summer day and splash and roll about. Sometimes one will even do a back flip, turning over completely to wash its back.

After the bath, the young geese dry off in the sunshine. But before long they're back in the water again, poking their heads below the surface in search of tasty water plants. Like most young birds, baby geese have BIG appetites.

When not bobbing like little corks on the water, baby geese can most likely be found enjoying a snack along the water's edge.

Waterfowl Cousins

Geese are related to ducks and swans. They are all part of an order of birds known as *waterfowl,* or birds that swim. Waterfowl are alike in many ways. They all have short legs and tails, and strong necks and wings.

Most waterfowl *migrate*—twice a year, they fly between feeding grounds in the North and nesting grounds in the South. Their bodies are streamlined for the long distances they fly between their two homes.

If you look at the feet of any waterfowl, you'll see that they're *webbed*—the toes are joined together by flaps of skin. Somewhat like rubber swimming flippers, the webbed feet help the birds to swim and dive.

Many birds nest in trees, but ducks, swans, and geese build their nests on the ground. But if their nests were in trees, these birds would not be able to get to their young. Each year, soon after their eggs have *hatched,* or produced young, all of these types of birds lose their flight feathers. None of them can fly until their new feathers grow in.

Big Goose, Little Goose

There are several different types of Canada Geese, but they all have a black head and white patches on their cheeks. You can tell the different types apart by their size, voice, and color. The biggest types of Canada Geese may weigh as much as a small child. They have deep voices and their necks are long. The smaller types have shorter necks, higher voices, and may weigh only as much as a cat.

Each type of Canada Goose has its own special *habitat,* or area in which it lives. For example, some types prefer marshy coastal areas, while others live in the tundra of northern Canada. A *tundra* is the flat, treeless area of the Arctic. And wherever you travel in central and western Canada, you'll probably find at least one type of Canada Goose.

You may be surprised to learn that not all Canada Geese live in Canada. Some types live in the northern United States.

The fine neck feathers of these giant honkers glisten like satin in the bright sunlight.

A Gorgeous Goose

It's difficult to tell a male goose, called a *gander,* from a female goose, but the female tends to be slightly smaller than the male. Both have gleaming feather coats. As geese strut about, they almost seem to enjoy showing off their feathers and spend a lot of time taking care of them. This is called *preening,* and geese do it every day.

Part of preening is oiling the feathers. Using its bill, the goose collects oil from a gland under its tail. A *gland* is a part of an animal's body that makes and gives out a substance. The goose then spreads this oil over all of its feathers. The oil keeps the feathers from drying out and breaking. Most important, this oil helps the goose's coat shed water while the goose is swimming or in the rain.

Though these Canada Geese appear to be dancing, they are actually preening.

Fantastic Feathers

The goose's handsome coat is made of several kinds of feathers. Along the edge of the wings are long, strong flight feathers. Covering its back are feathers that shed water very well and keep the goose's body dry.

Underneath these outer feathers are small fluffy feathers called *down*. They don't have a *shaft*—the hard part down the middle—and so they're very soft. The down feathers keep the goose warm in chilly weather by trapping warm air next to the body. If you've every slept in a down-filled sleeping bag, you know how cozy that can be.

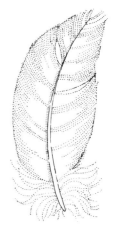

Outer feather

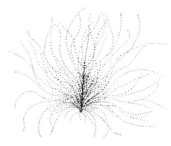

Down feather

A Canada Goose uses its down feathers to line its nest.

Powerful Wings

A Canada Goose usually flies at a speed of about 40 miles (65 kilometers) an hour. That's faster than a car travels on a city street. And a goose on a long flight can fly as high in the sky as some airplanes do.

A goose doesn't use its wings only for flying. When it is running, it keeps its wings stretched out for balance. By doing this, the goose can move along at an amazing speed. Its wings are powerful, too, and they can be used as weapons when the goose needs to protect itself or its young.

When being chased, a Canada Goose can fly at speeds of up to 60 miles (96 kilometers) an hour.

Bottoms Up

A goose eats about half a pound (one-quarter kilogram) of food a day. It likes grass, grains, berries, corn, and other wild plants.

It uses its long neck to search for food underwater. Like its duck cousins, the goose looks as if it's standing on its head when it's looking for food underwater. All you can see is its white rump sticking up out of the water.

When a goose scoops up underwater plants, it also gets a mouthful of water. Little toothlike spikes around its bill let the water drain out. The tip of a goose's bill is very sensitive to touch. It's used for feeling around underwater for food, as well as for spreading oil on its feathers.

As the geese fly south for the winter, they often stop at corn or grain fields to eat the stubble and plants left over from the harvest. Sometimes geese chase after insects in the field. A juicy bug is a great treat for a goose.

Canada Geese feed on water plants in lakes and ponds.

Super Senses

Many animals would like to catch a goose for dinner, so a goose needs to see and hear well in order to stay alive. If you were to sneak up on a *flock,* or large group, of geese, you would soon discover just how good geese's hearing is. At the first crack of a twig or rustle of leaves, the flock would fly off.

No one has yet been able to measure how sharp a goose's eyesight is, but scientists think it's probably very good. Sometimes a goose on the ground will look up into the sky and start calling. The sky looks empty, but in a few minutes a flock of geese will appear. The goose has seen them long before we could.

A goose's eyes are on the sides of its head, so it has to turn its head to see objects in front of it.

Gabby Goose

If you've ever heard a flock of Canada Geese flying overhead and honking, you probably remember the remarkable sound. The Canada Goose is one of the loudest birds around.

Opposite page:
A hissing goose's message is clear: STAY AWAY!

The Cree Indians call Canada Geese "the hounds of heaven" because their honking sounds like the barking of hound dogs. Some scientists believe geese stay together in their flocks by "talking" to each other all the time.

Geese make different sounds at different times. The honk is usually heard when they're flying. Special *vocal chords,* the part of the body that produces sound, and a very long neck enable geese to make this unusual honking sound.

If you meet a Canada Goose on the ground, the sound to watch out for is a hiss. A hissing goose extends its neck, opens its mouth wide, and spreads its powerful wings. It's trying to look dangerous—and it is. Be sure to give a hissing goose lots of room!

Migration Mysteries

In the fall, Canada Geese migrate south to warmer climates and head back north in the spring. How do all those geese find their way? No one knows for sure.

Some scientists believe that geese use the moon, sun, and stars to guide them. Others believe that geese sense and are guided by the direction of Earth's magnetic field. Only one thing is certain: millions of Canada Geese somehow do manage to find their way south every fall and back north every spring.

Canada Geese often fly in formation—in a big *V* shape, or sometimes in a long line, like a string of loose beads. At the front of each *V*-formation is a lead goose. The lead goose is "breaking trail" through the air just as you might break a trail through the snow. This makes flying easier for the geese following behind. From time to time, another goose takes over the lead so that one goose doesn't get too tired.

Opposite page: *Geese are not the only birds that fly in formation. Ducks and pelicans do, too. But you can always tell geese by their loud honks. The other birds fly silently.*

Highways in the Sky

Do you have a special route that you always follow to get from your house to a friend's home? Canada Geese have such favorite routes when they migrate. Although some geese can be seen migrating over most parts of the United States, they often use one of four main "highways" in the sky, called *flyways*. These flyways go from northern Canada to the coast of the Gulf of Mexico.

The four flyways are: the Atlantic, and the Pacific, which follow the coasts; the Mississippi, which follows the river; and the Central, which follows the Rocky Mountains. All four have areas of water and food where the geese stop year after year.

As many as a hundred geese may fly south together in a flock. They often fly for many hours without stopping. Flocks of geese land only when they're tired or hungry—or when the weather is bad.

Flocks of migrating geese fill the sky each spring and fall.

A Dangerous Trip

During the long flight south, the flock faces many dangers. Rain and hailstones slow the geese down, and fall is hunting season. All along the route, hunters wait for the geese to pass overhead. With all of these dangers, many of the geese never make it.

There are some places along the routes where hunting is not allowed. These marshy areas have many lakes and plenty of food for the tired and hungry geese. The geese seem to know where these safe spots are and land on them every year.

Winter Homes

By the time the geese reach their winter homes in the South, they've lost weight because of all the flying they've done. They'll spend most of the winter resting and putting on weight. The geese must build up a good layer of fat to be ready for the long flight north in the spring.

Choosing a Mate

Two- and three-year-old geese choose mates while they're in the South for the winter. Since Canada Geese mate for life, older geese already have partners. An older goose chooses a new mate only if its mate has died.

Scientists have observed a gander spend as much as three days looking over a group of females before deciding which one to pursue. Then he tries to get her away from the flock. But it's the female who makes the final choice. If she isn't interested, she ignores her pursuer, or tries to shoo him away.

Sometimes, if two ganders have their eye on the same female, they will fight. The angry ganders stretch their necks straight out like spears and charge, hissing loudly and flapping their wings. If one doesn't back off, they may hit each other with the bony edges of their wings and snap at each other with their bills.

When the fighting is over and the female has chosen her mate, the goose pair stretch their necks up and down and honk loudly. From now on, they will always be together.

Opposite page: *Out-honked and out-hissed, this unwelcome gander will have to look elsewhere for a mate.*

31

Back Home To Nest

Opposite page:
A raised nest site gives the protective goose mother an excellent view of the marsh.

Late in March, the days grow longer and the goose and the gander grow restless. It's time for them to go back to the place where they themselves were born, and to *mate,* or come together to produce young.

Their first job when they arrive back at their summer home is to choose a place to make a nest. They choose the place very carefully. The goose and the gander mate in the water and usually nest near the water, too. The favorite spots are marshy places or small islands in a lake or pond. But sometimes a pair builds a nest away from a lake, in a wet, spongy area called a *bog.*

Although geese are friendly birds and travel together in big flocks, the mother and father goose seem to like to be alone when they're nesting. They prefer not to have geese living right next door. But they don't seem to mind if a duck family moves into the neighborhood!

Sometimes, two pairs of geese fight over a nesting area. Both pairs honk and hiss until one leaves to find another nesting spot.

Getting to Work

The female goose builds the nest. She pulls together a pile of twigs and marsh grasses with her bill. Then she makes a nice rounded hole in the top of the pile with her body. Finally she plucks soft, warm down feathers from her chest to make a cozy lining for the nest.

The mother goose usually lays between three and eight creamy-white eggs. After each egg is laid, she pulls more feathers from her chest until she has a bare spot on her skin. She then presses this bare skin against the eggs to keep them warm. Periodically, she turns the eggs over with her bill to keep the temperature of the eggs even.

Within a month of being laid, these goose eggs will produce four fluffy babies.

Waiting—and Watching

For 25 to 30 days, the mother goose sits on her eggs. A goose father doesn't take turns on the nest as some bird fathers do. Instead, he stands guard, making sure no egg-stealers get near the nest. If he senses danger he flies into the air, honking loudly to frighten the intruder. Sometimes he may even attack, hissing, biting, and flapping his wings ferociously. Although there are many animals that might like to have a tasty goose egg for dinner, few will take on this angry parent.

The female doesn't leave the nest. Instead, she crouches low over it so that she and her nest will not be seen by *predators,* animals that hunt other animals for food.

Happy Hatchday

When the eggs are ready to hatch, little peeps, cheeps, and tap-tapping sounds come from inside the eggs. This is the way a baby goose, called a *gosling* (GAHZ-ling), says, "I'm ready to come out now!"

Egg tooth on a gosling's bill

Each gosling has a special, hard *egg tooth* on the top of its bill to help chip through its shell. First a small hole appears in the shell, followed by a crack. Breaking out of its shell is very hard work for a gosling, but the mother and father just stand by watching. The little gosling inside the egg might be hurt if the mother or father poked at the egg from the outside. Finally, a tiny bill pokes out through the shell. Then the gosling's head appears, with its eyes blinking at the bright new world.

After the wet little body is out of the shell, the gosling lies down to rest while its feathers dry. Within 24 hours, all its brothers and sisters will hatch, too. The newly hatched family is called a *clutch* of geese.

Overleaf:
A mother goose almost never leaves the nest— and the father never sits on it. His responsibility is to defend it, a job he performs fiercely.

Are You My Mother?

Unlike many other animal babies, a gosling doesn't know who its parents are when it is first born. It thinks that the first animal it sees is its parent. If a horse is the first animal a gosling sees after hatching, it will think that the horse is its parent! This is why the goose parents stay close to the nest. They are making sure that their babies see them first and will know them as their parents. *Imprinting* is the name given to the experience of a newborn of some animals to recognize the first object it sees as its parent.

Raring to Go

Within hours, the goslings leave the nest. And once they do, they never return to it.

The goslings' fluffy little bodies are an olive-yellow color. The babies change and grow quickly. Sometimes they double their weight in the first week of life. By the time they're two weeks old, the goslings turn gray, and their soft down begins to be covered by feathers. In six weeks they have black feathers, and their white cheek patches begin to show.

Opposite page:
Hatched in a downy nest with its mother looking on, this gosling has imprinted on the goose and will always recognize her as its parent.

Growing Up

Opposite page:
Swimming is one of the first and most important lessons a gosling must learn. And the babies have usually mastered the skill by the time they're just a few days old.

One of the first lessons goslings must learn is how to swim. To do that, they have to get to the water. Most of the time the nest is close by, and the goslings don't have to go very far. But sometimes if a nest is far from water, the goose family reaches it by walking single file in a straight line. The mother leads the way, the goslings follow her, and the father brings up the rear. The little balls of fluff march behind their mother, crossing busy roads and climbing up and down over rocks, logs, and hills—all to get to water.

During the summer months, the goslings eat and grow. They learn by copying what their parents do. The young learn what food to look for and where to find it. They practice tipping upside down to find food underwater. And they learn the danger signs—the sign of a fox in the grass or the sight of a hawk circling in the sky. Even a one-day-old gosling is able to get away from danger by diving and swimming underwater for more than 30 feet (10 meters).

Opposite page:
While the geese's flight feathers are growing in, tall grasses help provide necessary cover for grounded goose families.

Grounded!

Every year at the same time, when the goslings are half grown, the mother and father lose the big feathers on their wings and tail. Losing one set of feathers and growing another is called *molting*. During this time, the adult geese cannot fly, but they aren't helpless. They still run across the water flapping their wings to speed them along.

Learning To Fly

By the time the parents' new feathers have grown in, the goslings are ready to learn to fly. The babies seem to know how to fly so they don't need much teaching. Their first flights are short ones, but soon they follow their parents to new feeding grounds.

By the time the young Canada Geese are eight weeks old, they are fully grown and hard to tell apart from their parents. The young may now be 25 times bigger than they were at birth. If people grew that fast, an eight-week-old baby would weigh as much as a grown man!

Summer's End

At the end of summer, the goose family leaves the nesting area and moves to a new feeding ground. There, they are joined by other goose families looking for food.

When the flock is feeding, there is one goose, called a *sentinel,* that stands guard. The others munch happily on marsh grasses and pondweeds. The sentinel often finds a high spot of land where it can see all around, bending its flexible neck in all directions. If the sentinel senses danger, it honks loudly to warn the others.

Time To Go South Again

As summer turns to fall, the weather turns colder and the grasses and weeds dry out and die. Once again, the geese become restless. The shorter days warn them that winter is coming. They start to gather in large groups for the long flight south to their winter home. When you hear their honks and see their *V*-formations in the sky, you will also know that winter is coming.

Words To Know

Bog   An area with wet spongy ground.

Clutch   Eggs laid by a bird, and the babies that hatch from them.

Down   A bird's very soft, fluffy feathers.

Egg tooth   A toothlike point on the tip of a baby goose's bill used to help the baby crack out of its shell.

Flock   A large group of birds that lives and feeds together.

Flyways   Special routes that birds follow on their migrations.

Gaggle   A flock of geese, especially on the ground.

Gander   A male goose.

Gland   The animal body part that makes and gives out a substance.

Gosling   A young goose.

Habitat   The area in which an animal or plant naturally lives.

Hatch   To break out of an egg.

Imprinting   The name given to the experience of some animals in which a newborn recognizes the first animal it sees as its parent.

Mate   To come together to produce young.

Migrate   To move from one place to another.

Molt   To lose one set of feathers and grow another.

Predator   An animal that hunts other animals for food.

Preening   Cleaning, smoothing, and oiling the feathers.

Sentinel   A look-out bird that guards a feeding flock.

Shaft   The hard stem down the middle of a feather.

Tundra   Flat land in the Arctic where no trees grow.

Waterfowl   Birds that swim.

Webbed feet   Feet with toes that are joined together by flaps of skin.

Vocal chords   The body part that produces sound.

Index

PHOTO CREDITS
Cover: Robert McCaw, *Ivy Images.* **Interiors:** *Ivy Images:* Bill Ivy, 4, 8, 11, 13, 14, 17, 21, 22, 29, 30, 41, 43, 45; Robert McCaw, 33. */Visuals Unlimited:* Glenn M. Oliver, 7; William J. Weber, 18; Tom Edwards, 24. */Maslowski Photo:* 26. */Network Stock Photo File:* Barry Griffiths, 34, 45.

Getting To Know...

Nature's Children

HIPPOPOTAMUSES

Sally Banks

SCHOLASTIC INC.

New York   Toronto   London   Auckland   Sydney
Mexico City   New Delhi   Hong Kong   Buenos Aires

Facts in Brief

Classification of the Hippopotamus

Class: *Mammalia* (mammals)

Order: *Artiodactyla*

Family: *Hippopotamidae*

Genus: *Hippopotamus* (common hippopotamus)
Choeropsis (pygmy hippopotamus)

Species: *Hippopotamus amphibius* (common hippopotamus)
Choeropsis liberiensis (pygmy hippopotamus)

World distribution. Africa

Habitat. Varies with species.

Distinctive physical characteristics. Have large, barrel-shaped body and short legs. Common hippo is gray-brown to blue-black; pygmy hippo is gray-black.

Habits. Common hippo lives near water in groups of up to 100; usually spends the day in water; goes on land to feed at night. Pygmy hippo lives alone or in pairs and spends more time on land than the common hippo.

Diet. Vegetation.

Published by Scholastic Inc.
90 Old Sherman Turnpike, Danbury, Connecticut 06816.

SCHOLASTIC and associated logos are trademarks and/or registered trademarks of Scholastic Inc.

ISBN: 0-7172-7741-0   Printed in the U.S.A.

Photo Rights: Ivy Images   *Cover Design:* Niemand Design

Have you ever wondered . . .

Long ago, travelers in Africa thought hippos were monsters. These "monsters" lived in lakes, rivers, and streams. They had huge, barrel-shaped bodies, short legs, and gigantic mouths. Sometimes, these creatures hid below the surface of the water, and other times, they reared up out of the water and tipped over boats.

They made a lot of strange noises, too. They would grunt, growl, roar, and scream. Sometimes they would even moo like a cow and neigh like a horse.

Perhaps these sounds are why people named the creature the hippopotamus, which means "river horse." Today we know that a hippo isn't a monster. It also isn't related to horses. Just what kind of animal *is* a hippopotamus? Read more to find out.

A hippo opens its mouth wide to scare away other animals as well as other male hippos.

Opposite page:
*The shy pygmy
hippo is much
smaller and more
timid than the
common hippo.*

Family Tree

If a hippo wanted to have a family reunion, it could invite its distant relatives—the pigs. But if it wanted to ask only its closest family members, it would be a small party. The hippo's only near relative is the smaller pygmy hippo.

Scientists now know that there were once several species, or types, of hippopotamuses. A million years ago, these hippos could be found throughout Europe, England, Africa, and China. Today the two surviving species of hippos are found in the wild only in parts of Africa.

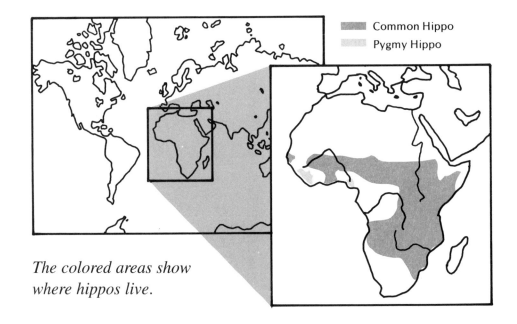

Common Hippo
Pygmy Hippo

*The colored areas show
where hippos live.*

Home to a Hippo

Hippos live in areas with plenty of water. Found in grasslands, rivers, and lakes, hippos spend most of the day in the water—swimming and sleeping. In fact, they lead rather lazy lives during the day.

But when darkness falls, hippos leave their watery homes and search for food on land. They usually travel no more than a couple of miles (a few kilometers) to feed. If they have to travel farther to find food, hippos rest and refresh themselves in shallow pools, called *wallows*. Then they continue their journey to look for food. Hippos feed for about five hours at night and then return to the water for a long nap.

Relaxing in or near water is a hippo's favorite way to spend the day.

Heavyweights

The hippopotamus is one of the heaviest land animals. Only the elephant and an occasional white rhinoceros weigh more than the hippo.

An adult male hippo, which is called a *bull,* may weigh more than 6,600 pounds (almost 3,000 kilograms). You certainly wouldn't want one to step on your foot! From its nose to its tail, a bull is about 15 feet (4.5 meters) long and it stands 5 feet (1.5 meters) tall. A female hippo, called a *cow,* is a bit smaller.

The hippo enjoys sunning itself for short periods of time.

Big Yet Fast

Hippopotamuses have very big heads and large round bodies. Their bellies nearly touch the ground because of their short, stubby legs. These huge animals have four toes on each foot. The toes are joined together by thick skin and are protected by round, black "toenails," which are really nail-like hooves.

In spite of its enormous size, a hippo can run on land as fast as a person can. And a hippo can move even faster in the water.

A hippo may graze during the day but only for a short time and never far from the safety of water.

13

River Horses

Hippos move faster and more gracefully in the water than on land. Their special *webbed* toes— toes that are joined together by flaps of skin— help to make hippos excellent swimmers. Not only do they swim like dogs do, paddling with their feet, hippos also walk along the bottom of rivers and lakes.

Because hippos can submerge their bodies so that only their eyes, noses, and ears are above water, the animals can hardly be seen as they float in still or slow-moving water. Meanwhile, they can still see, breathe, and hear.

With their large lungs, hippos can spend up to 30 minutes underwater! As they dive, special muscles close their nostrils and fold down their ears to keep out the water. Then when the animals come to the surface again, they quickly wiggle their ears back and forth to shake them dry.

A hippo may spend up to 18 hours a day in the water.

Thick Skinned

Hippo skin is thick and tough. But the *epidermis,* which is the outer layer of skin, is very thin. This is why a hippo spends much of its life in the water. Staying underwater during the day keeps the hippo's thin skin from drying out in the hot sun.

A sticky, red-brown liquid oozes from the hippo's special skin *glands.* A gland is a part of an animal's body that makes and gives out a substance. Because of the color of this liquid, people once thought that the hippo sweated blood. Scientists now know this isn't true. The liquid is simply an oily substance that helps to keep the hippo's skin healthy and prevent it from drying out and getting sunburned. Should a hippo become wounded, the reddish brown liquid also helps the animal's skin to heal quickly.

At first glance, the hippopotamus seems to be hairless. But in fact, it has tiny hairs scattered over most of its body. Longer and thicker hairs, called *bristles,* are found on its head and on the end of its short tail.

Water and a coating of mud keep a hippo cool in the blazing sun of its habitat, *the area where it lives in the wild.*

Hippo Helpers

Overleaf:
*Nap time in a
hippo nursery.*

You might not think that something as small
as a bird or a fish could be of much use to an
enormous hippo, but you would be surprised.
In fact, a number of different creatures help the
hippo, and it returns the favor.

Birds, such as egrets and wagtails, help
to keep the hippo healthy. These birds eat flies
and ticks off of the hippo's skin. Hungry fish
also do their part. They eat *algae,* which are tiny
water plants, that sometimes grow on a hippo.

In turn, hippos serve as safe perches where a
variety of birds can rest—out of reach of their
enemies. And young crocodiles and turtles often
find the backs of hippos the perfect place for
basking in the sun.

*Two friends watch out for one another among
the water cabbage.*

Getting the Message

Hippos often look as though they aren't paying any attention to what is going on around them. But in reality, their small, round ears can pick up even the softest of sounds. Hippos also have an excellent sense of smell. But no one knows for sure how well hippos see. Some people believe the animals see quite well, while others think hippos can only see clearly things that are very close to them.

Although the hippo is usually quiet, it makes a range of sounds, depending on how the animal feels. An angry hippo roars or bellows. An excited hippo neighs like a horse. When a cow is looking for a *mate,* or partner, she makes a mooing sound. And a pair of fighting bulls will often shriek and squeal.

Even when relaxing, a hippo stays alert to potential danger.

Teeth and Tusks

When it comes to teeth, a hippo has a mouthful. It has 38 to 42 large, strong teeth while humans have only 32.

The hippo's molars are far back in its mouth. Used for chewing and grinding up food, the molars wear down as a hippo ages.

A hippo's biggest teeth are its canines, which are called *tusks,* and they never stop growing. In fact, a tusk of one hippo measured 25 inches (63.5 centimeters) long! A bull's tusks are much larger than a cow's. A male uses his tusks to fight other bulls.

A hippo's tusks, like an elephant's, are made of ivory. But unlike the elephant's tusks, the hippo's huge teeth fit *inside* its mouth when it is closed. And a hippo's tusks grow out of the animal's lower jaw, while an elephant's tusks are part of its upper jaw.

A hippo's tusks are strong enough to crush an adult crocodile.

Hungry Hippos

Although hippos are big, you aren't likely to see them munching much. Why? Because during the day, they spend most of the time snoozing on sandbars or wallowing in the water, sometimes nibbling on water plants.

When it gets dark, though, hippos leave the protection of the water and travel onto land. Following well-worn trails that the animals have used for many, many years, hippos may walk great distances to find food.

Hippos are *herbivores,* which means they eat plants. Their favorite food is marsh grass. Hippos can eat almost 90 pounds (40 kilograms) of food in one night. Although this may sound like a lot, hippos actually eat less than many other animals of similar size. Hippopotamuses simply don't need as much food because of their calm way of life.

If a hippo feels threatened, it retreats to the water.

A Herd of Hippos

Female hippos love company and live together in a *herd,* which is also called a school. A large herd may contain as many as 100 cows and their babies, called *calves.* A group of females leads each herd.

The bulls live around the outside of the herd. Each bull has his own *territory,* called a *refuge,* where the bull lives. Many bull refuges surround each herd.

A female will travel back and forth between its herd and any refuge, but a male cannot simply stroll into a herd. If a male wants to enter, he must get permission from the females. If he doesn't behave properly, the females will attack him and drive him away.

Cows usually travel in herds of between 10 to 20 cows and their calves.

Getting Along

Despite their huge size, most hippos are peaceful animals. They don't usually attack other animals or humans unless the hippos feel they're in danger.

Cows and calves get along well together. They seldom fight and regularly sleep side by side and relax together in the water.

But bulls behave quite differently. They often fight with each other. The strongest bulls live in the refuges closest to the herd. Old, weak, and young bulls live farther away from the cows and calves. Young bulls have to fight their way to the herd if they want to mate, or come together to produce young.

A fight between two bulls may last for hours.

Yawning Mad

Just like you, a hippo yawns when it's tired. But when a bull opens his mouth wide enough to show all his teeth, he's telling another male to back away. If the intruder doesn't move, the defender bull rears up out of the water and rushes forward. Then he may blow water through his nostrils and charge forward again.

This is usually enough to convince the intruder to go away. But if not, a fight begins. Both bulls rush at each other with their mouths open, splashing water in all directions. The males slash at each other with their big tusks. The tusks are fierce weapons that can easily cut open and punch holes in the hippos' skin, which is why male hippos are often covered with wounds and scars.

Injuries from a fight are often serious. Some bulls may even fight until one is killed.

"Back off or else!"

Getting Together

When female hippos are five to seven years old, they are old enough to mate and produce calves. Young males who want to mate, though, will have to fight older bulls for a spot near the herd. It may take young males several years to get such a spot. Although males fight each other for the chance to mate with the females, the cows make the final decision.

Mating may take place at any time of the year. The cow and the bull usually mate in the water.

The calf is born about eight months later, often during the wettest time of the year. A lot of rain means a lot of grass. This is important because the mother needs to eat extra food to produce plenty of milk for her calf.

With the herd nearby, a cow and her calf spend much time nuzzling.

Water Babies

When a mother hippo is ready to have her baby, she goes off alone and hunts for a safe and sheltered spot. Sometimes she has her calf on land. Other times, a mother gives birth underwater.

If the calf is born in the water, it quickly paddles to the surface for its first breath of air. A newborn hippo can only stay underwater for about 20 to 30 seconds. It takes some time for a baby hippo to learn to hold its breath longer.

The newborn calf weighs more than an average eight-year-old child. The calf stands about 1.5 feet (half a meter) high and measures about 3 feet (about 1 meter) in length from the tip of its nose to the tip of its tail.

A cow swims alongside her four-week-old calf.

Getting Around

A baby hippo can walk, run, and swim just a few minutes after it is born. A calf born in the water learns to swim before it learns to walk. The calf can drink milk from its mother both underwater and on land. A mother hippo nurses her calf for eight months.

The cow and her calf stay by themselves for two weeks. When the calf is strong enough, they return to the herd. After that, when the mother wants to eat, she leaves her baby with the other cows. They baby-sit the young hippo until its mother returns.

Mother and baby spend a lot of time in and near the water. When the calf gets tired, it crawls up for a restful ride on its mother's back as she floats around. This is also the safest place for the youngster in case there are any crocodiles nearby.

Hitching a ride.

Absolutely No Wandering Allowed

The first year of life for hippo calves is a dangerous time. Even though adult hippos don't have many enemies, baby hippos do. Not only do crocodiles attack calves in the water, lions and hyenas hunt them on land. So mother hippos are always on alert and will fiercely attack any animal—besides other cows—that comes too close to her young.

Because a calf's life is at risk, a mother hippo has to teach her baby quickly to stay close to her at all times. The minute a calf starts to stray, the mother punishes it. She might roll the calf over, hit the baby with her head, or swat at it with her tusks. Once the calf obeys her, the mother cuddles it and licks it with her tongue.

In order to protect her baby, a mother hippo is constantly aware of other approaching animals.

Growing Up

As calves grow larger, they begin to play with other young hippos in the herd. They tumble together on land and splash about in the water.

When the young are about four or five months old, they begin to eat grass and other plants. The calves are finally strong enough to follow their mothers to their herds' favorite feeding grounds.

Young cows stay with the herd. Young bulls, however, leave the herd when they are about one year old.

Because the older bulls already occupy the territories nearby, a young male has to go beyond these refuges to find his own spot. As he gets older and stronger, he will fight to win a territory close to the herd.

A mother allows playful behavior from her calf.

The Pygmy Hippopotamus

The pygmy is much smaller than the common hippo. But the pygmy still weighs up to 600 pounds (272 kilograms)—about as much as four adult humans. A pygmy stands about 3 feet (about 1 meter) tall at the shoulder and is typically 5 to 6 feet (1.5 to 2 meters) long.

It lives in forests near water and in swamps, eating plants as well as fruit that it finds on the ground. Because the pygmy spends less time in the water than the common hippo, the pygmy's feet are less webbed.

Besides their size, one of the most remarkable differences between pygmy and common hippos is that pygmies live alone or in pairs. They are very shy animals and often hide in forests or in the water.

Seven months after mating, a pygmy mother gives birth to one calf. A pygmy calf usually weighs about 9 pounds (4 kilograms) at birth. Weeks pass before a baby pygmy learns to walk.

By five months old, a pygmy calf will weigh 10 times more than it did at birth.

Helping the Hippo

Long ago, hippos lived in most parts of Africa, wherever there was enough water. For centuries, people hunted hippos for meat, for their ivory tusks, and for sport.

Today hippos are faced with an even greater danger than hunters. More and more parts of Africa are being turned into farms and ranches. This means there is less land for hippopotamuses and other wild animals.

So man has created protected parks and *game preserves,* where most hippos now live. Even though laws have been passed to stop people from killing hippos, the gentle giants need special help if more than a few small herds are to survive.

Words To Know

Algae   Tiny plants that grow in the water.

Bristles   The long, thick hairs on a hippo's head and tail.

Bull   A male hippopotamus.

Calf   A young hippopotamus.

Cow   A female hippopotamus.

Epidermis   The outer layer of the skin.

Game preserve   A place where animals are protected from being hunted.

Gland   The animal body part that makes and gives out a substance.

Habitat   The area in which an animal or plant naturally lives.

Herbivore   A plant-eating animal.

Herd   A group of female hippos and their calves; also called a school.

Mate   To come together to produce young. Either member of an animal pair is also the other's mate.

Nurse   To drink milk from a mother's body.

Refuge   The territory protected by a male hippo.

Territory   An area that an animal, or a group of animals, lives in and often defends from other animals of the same kind.

Tusks   The special pointed teeth found in the mouths of some animals, such as hippos and elephants.

Wallows   Shallow pools where hippos rest.

Webbed toes   Toes that are joined together by flaps of skin.

Index

PHOTO CREDITS

Cover: Spectrum Stock, *Ivy Images.* **Interiors:** *Ivy Images:* Bill Ivy, 7, 11, 32; M. Beedell, 15; Alan and Sandy Carey, 19, 31, 39; Hot Shots, 16, 24; Bill Lowry, 44; Len Rue Jr., 8, 35; Spectrum Stock, 20, 42; D. Taylor, 12, 28, 36, 40; M. Turco, 23, 27; Philip van den Berg, 4.

The Carnegie Public Library
202 N. Animas St., Trinidad, CO.
(719) 846-6841

1 2 3 4 5 6 7 8 9 10 11 12 **2013**	1
7-7-15	